Endorsements

Working in a ministry that targets men, it's refreshing to discover new material that introduces men to great devotionals. Todd's new *40 Days in the Man Cave* does just that! The message of men needing to get away to a place where they can be re-energized is fantastic! I believe all men would benefit from reading *40 Days in the Man Cave*!

–Norm Bishop
Director of Men's Ministry, Western Ontario District PAOC
Burlington, Ontario

I have had the privilege of knowing Todd for the past twenty years. He is a man of integrity who walks humbly before the Lord.

It's been said that the place of your greatest pain can become the place for your greatest potential, your greatest purpose. This is certainly true of Todd. As he looks back on times spent in his own cave, Todd shares how there is *devastation* in every place in life. God wants to bring a *manifestation*.

In his book, *40 Days in the Man Cave*, Todd reminds men that we were meant to be overcomers. Each devotional provides the encouragement men need to walk in victory.

–Rev. Nathan Albrecht
FGT Family Church
Leamington, Ontario

Appreciate Todd's efforts in challenging guys to be quiet and still each day, to pause and reflect and listen, then make adjustments and move ahead with energy and excitement for what lies ahead.

–Mark Osborne
Former 14 year NHL player
Current Hockey Ministries International NHL Rep

I give Todd Stahl's *Man Cave* a 10/10!

–Tim Arkell
Calgary, Alberta

A man needs another man to talk to him about the deep stuff. We have enough trouble hearing, enough struggle listening, enough resistance to responding, that unless another man clamps our shoulders, looks us square in the eyes, and gives us the straight goods, we could run from ourselves the whole day long. Todd Stahl is that man, and *40 Days in the Man Cave* is that straight talk. It's clear, fair, honest, and true. Have a listen yourself.

–Mark Buchanan
Author of *Your Church is Too Safe*

40 Days in the

MAN CAVE

MEN'S DEVOTIONAL

Todd Stahl

40 DAYS IN THE MAN CAVE
Copyright © 2015 by Todd Stahl

Printed in Canada

ISBN: 978-1-4866-0858-4

Word Alive Press
131 Cordite Road, Winnipeg, MB R3W 1S1
www.wordalivepress.ca

WORD ALIVE
—P R E S S—

FSC

MIX
Paper from
responsible sources
www.fsc.org   FSC® C016245

Stahl, Todd, 1968-, author
    40 days in the man cave : men's devotional / Todd Stahl.

Issued in print and electronic formats.
ISBN 978-1-4866-0858-4 (pbk.).--ISBN 978-1-4866-0859-1 (pdf).--
ISBN 978-1-4866-0860-7 (html).--ISBN 978-1-4866-0861-4 (epub)

    1. Christian men--Religious life. 2. Christian men--Prayers and devotions. 3. Christian life--Meditations. I. Title. II. Title: Forty days in the man cave.

BV4528.2.S73 2015   248.8'42   C2015-900778-X
                                             C2015-900779-8

Acknowledgments

A very big thank you to all my family and friends for your thoughts, valuable input, and belief in me!

To my wife Sherry (Fletch) for her massive dose of daily encouragement, resilience, and full confidence that *Man Cave* would become a reality.

Thank you to God for fixing my heart in more ways than one.

My prayer for the guys reading *40 Days in the Man Cave* is that this book gets as much use as those nasty shoes you cut the lawn with and can't seem to get rid of!

It's time to enter the cave...

Introduction

Very early in the morning, while it was still dark, Jesus got up, left the house and went off to a solitary place, where he prayed.

–Mark 1:35, NIV

Jesus needed a man cave! If even Jesus knew this was a necessity, no wonder guys follow His lead.

Numerous times in scripture, we read about Jesus looking for a sanctuary to get away from people and be alone. Jesus had the same emotions we feel every day. His days weren't all picnics. There were times when He was overwhelmed, tired, frustrated, angry, and simply required some space.

The key is that Jesus recognized there was safety in the cave. This was a hideaway where he could regain His strength. Here He could turn for direction and guidance.

Whether you're worn out or simply need a breather, where is that place for you? What emotions draw you to your cave? Nowadays men are bombarded with expectations at work, our church, and in our homes. We are expected to be leaders. Guys don't want to show their flaws.

Hey, you can try and go it alone, and life may run like a well-oiled machine, but sooner or later you're going to mess up or make a bad decision. When these circumstances arise, having a sanctuary–or man cave–is vital. This is a place where you and God can hang out and talk. A place where He can teach us and have our full attention.

Some guys go to the cave for the wrong reasons. Or worse, they go to a cave they should not be in. They're not willing to deal with reality. They want to shut the world out. A man cave is meant to be like a gas station to refuel, or an outlet to re-charge the batteries.

For me, personally, I've had some tough years when I "craved the cave." I desperately needed a place to hide, escape, and feel peace. During a difficult and challenging time in my life, I lived in a two-bedroom apartment with my kids. This left me sleeping on a well-worn pullout couch in the living room every night. We had hockey blankets covering the windows, and a stove that didn't work. Factor in neighbors across the street that cranked Spanish music like a Mexican fiesta till the early hours most nights!

Guess what? My son nicknamed the apartment our "man cave." Although this place didn't feel like home for my kids, words cannot describe how that apartment absolutely became my sanctuary. My cave. I learned so much, and my spiritual growth really developed out of the adversity.

We all have to choose. Are we going to be bitter or better? When you carve time out of your day to meet with God on a regular basis, your life will inevitably change for the better. I was confronted with a lot of difficult situations. I'm sure that as you read these pages, you may be staring at some big challenges. During those months in the apartment, my cousin Judy gave me a plaque which read "When it is dark enough, you can see the stars."

Find your cave. Include God. Relax. Seek His direction. And in the midst of the quiet darkness, the stars will appear and recharge your faith.

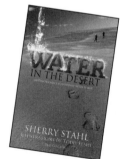

Join the community! Sign up on takethe40daychallenge.com for encouragement along the way!

Know someone else who should try The 40 Day Challenge? Meet the women's counterpart to *40 Days in the Man Cave: Water in the Desert* by Sherry Stahl! Learn more on page 95.

God holds me head and shoulders above all who try to pull me down...
Already I'm singing God-songs; I'm making music to God.

—PSALM 27:6

Many times in my life, I have given too much thought to background noise. Those voices attempt to make you think aspects of your life are falling apart. You anticipate that the future will be a scary place, or the walls feel as if they're pressing in on you like a vice. Do not allow those sounds to be played. God has provided courage and faith to confront your fear and anxiety.

Nehemiah, a mighty man in the Bible, encountered an excellent example of this dilemma. At a time when he could have been comfortable with his highly honored position of cupbearer for the king, God spoke to him, confirming that he would be the lead man to reconstruct the walls around the city of Jerusalem.

During the physical work, Nehemiah heard sounds of criticism, verbal attacks, and false accusations day in and day out. Nehemiah refused to listen. He kept his focus. Not only did he refuse to crumble to the background noise, he and his construction crew completed the job in record time!

Don't be surprised if the devil starts heating up the adversity when you pursue a goal that God has confirmed in your heart. In your own life, scrub away those words or thoughts that have held you back from spiritual growth. Listen for the voice of encouragement. Open your spiritual ears to hear what God is saying to you today.

The enemy desires nothing better than to play the sounds of negativity, doubt, and confusion in our minds, hoping we'll lose focus. These words are attempts to smother the dreams God placed in us to fulfill. Turn off the old playlist of doubt and fear. Download the new sounds God has given to you—lyrics of hope, anticipation, and excitement towards a future that is music to your hears!

HEBREWS 10: 33-39
ISAIAH 12:2
LUKE 6:22-23
PROVERBS 12:25

WHAT DREAM HAVE YOU WANTED TO PURSUE THAT IS COLLECTING DUST
OR HAS BEEN NEGLECTED DUE TO FEAR?

Devotion Two:
SAND IN YOUR SHOE

For God is pleased with you when you do what you know is right and patiently endure unfair treatment.

—1 Peter 2:19, NLT

If you ever go for a run to burn off that loaded bacon cheeseburger, you can get such a terrible irritation from a few simple grains of sand in your shoe. Eventually the sand rubs against your skin to the point where it becomes unbearable to keep moving. However, if you take that same grain of sand and add it to an oyster shell, the result over time will create a beautiful pearl!

How can something as tiny as a grain of sand get between the shell and the oyster? The oyster doesn't like that sand in its shell any more than we cannot stand having something irritating in our lives. An oyster will secrete a substance called nacre to get rid of the sand. The longer the process of secretion goes on, the bigger the pearl will be! The same holds true in our lives. We all have "sand" that can wear us down and cause friction. The flip side is that the sand will eventually produce something miraculous in our lives.

In 2008, with the encouragement of my daughter, the two of us went on a mission trip to Guatemala. We agree that this trip impacted our lives in a massive way. A teenage Guatemalan girl gave a powerful testimony which left a lasting impression on me. At such a young age, she had already gone through difficulties most people don't experience in their lifetime. With tears in her eyes and intense passion, she spoke of the terrible hardship and criticism she had received from her family for giving her life to Christ. One night while praying, God spoke to her so clearly. One sentence clearly stood out. God said to her, "You are my pearl." She had us all captivated by her story. I sat there speechless. In that moment, I recognized that God had made a beautiful pearl from this young girl's sand.

What in your life has been an irritation that formed something good? Do you trust God enough to believe He can and will work that sand into something great, even though right now all you feel is irritation?

ROMANS 8:26–30
1 PETER 3:14
1 PETER 4:16–19
2 CORINTHIANS 1:5

IS THERE A TIME IN YOUR LIFE WHEN YOU CAN RECOGNIZE THAT GOD HELPED YOU OVERCOME YOUR PAIN FOR A GREATER GAIN?

Devotion Three:
SECOND FIDDLE

John answered, "I only baptize using water. A person you don't recognize has taken his stand in your midst. He comes after me, but he is not in second place to me. I'm not even worthy to hold his coat for him."

—John 1:26-27

Some people are born leaders. Not all of us are called to be a leader, and that's okay! We all have God-given qualities to excel in life. The dictionary defines a second fiddle as "one that plays a supporting or subservient role."[1] Second fiddles are without question important. They provide key support and are a vital component.

In the Bible, Jonathan wasn't just one of David's best friends; he would definitely be considered a second fiddle. Jonathan was the heir to the throne, but he was willing to give it up in order for David to take the position. He was loyal, faithful, and willing to sacrifice his own gain.

How about John the Baptist? God called John the Baptist to fulfill the role of second fiddle. John understood his role and knew in his heart the significance of preparing the way for Jesus. To play second fiddle, you must be self-confident and unselfish. Second fiddle is definitely not second-class!

Imagine this scenario. You have tickets to a sold-out concert. People are mingling around, finding their seats. The orchestra has gathered and is awaiting the entrance of the lead vocalist. She is a stunning, beautiful blonde who captures the attention of everyone as she gracefully finds her place on stage. You begin to smirk as your eyes scan to the big fat guy in the back row of the orchestra, with his shirt untucked, waiting to blow on his tuba. Quite a contrast! He may play second fiddle to the vocalist, but she can't sing until that tuba bellows its notes!

Any musician will tell you that each instrument is equally important to the harmony of an orchestra. Many leaders would never attain success if not for the people who served as their second fiddles. John the Baptist knew his role was to step back in order for Jesus to move forward. However, both men played vital roles as they taught crowds of people who crammed together to listen.

You never know... playing second fiddle might just be what someone needs from you! If you support and encourage others, God will reward your faithfulness![2]

JOHN 3:26–30
PHILIPPIANS 2:3–4
MARK 10:41–45
ROMANS 12:10

CAN YOU THINK OF ANYONE RIGHT NOW WHO MAY NEED YOUR ENCOURAGEMENT,
OR SOMEONE WHO HAS PLAYED SECOND FIDDLE SO YOU COULD ACHIEVE YOUR GOAL?

Get rid of all bitterness, rage and anger...

—Ephesians 4:31, NIV

If you've ever been to court, you can agree with me that the whole ordeal is traumatic. There are lawyers, judges, and an emotional rollercoaster that leaves a lasting impression. Personally, I had this exact unfortunate experience. I was frustrated, upset, and hardly given the chance to be heard.

We all know how difficult it can be to listen as unjustified accusations are thrown at you like darts! Each time I had to return to the courtroom, a new judge was ruling on the same case. I became bitter, and a part of me wanted revenge. I was certainly showing signs of a crusty hardening of the heart.

Romans 12:19 says, *"Dear friends, never take revenge. Leave that to the righteous anger of God"* (NLT). I had to let God be my defender. Think about the men of the Bible—like Joseph, thrown into a pit and sold as a slave, or Paul, tossed in jail. They suffered for offences they never even committed! Despite the unfair treatment, they remained faithful. At the time, both circumstances looked bleak, yet God had a plan for their lives. He would use their adversity for good.

Once you let God be the judge, you take back your power and regain your peace. God promises in His word that He will vindicate you. Call on God, trust Him, and believe that in time He will make things right. Don't harden your heart.

I love the saying my grandfather scribbled in the back of his weathered bible: "The same SON that hardens the clay, melts the butter!" Our hearts and attitudes can get hard, or we can allow God to soften us up, and let the past be past at last!

It's all in how we look at things. Quit docking your boat in Bitterness Harbor, anchored to old events that leave you stuck, going absolutely nowhere. Ask God to release those old emotions and memories. Get free from the past and look forward to what God has in store for your life!

JOEL 2:25
ISAIAH 29:21
PROVERBS 28:14
ISAIAH 43:18-19

HOW WILL YOU CHANGE YOUR BITTERNESS TO FEEL A SENSE OF FREEDOM?

Devotion Five:
PUT AWAY YOUR SHOVEL

Can any of you by worrying add a single hour to your life?

—Matthew 6:27, NIV

Spring is a great time of year. For farmers all over the world, spring is the beginning of a new season. Their equipment is ready to go, the land gets cultivated, seed goes in the ground, and on they go to other jobs that require their attention. They wait, not worrying. A farmer relies on nature to takes its course. Do they stress about disease outbreak, too much rain, too little rain, an early frost, or extreme heat? No. They wait. Farmers must learn to trust.

I often think about the saying, "Whatever you plant in faith, don't dig up in doubt." This is such a good reminder. If a farmer walked out into the field and unearthed the seed with his or her boot to check if the crop was growing, wouldn't that be ridiculous? The same is true for our lives. When you plant seeds deep in your soul, the roots will get into the rich, fertilized soil—and the result will produce plenty of healthy fruit. If we just scratch the top layer of soil to plant the seeds, they aren't going to get into the ground and soak up the nutrients they need to grow.

This is similar to setting aside time with God and allowing spiritual development in our lives. When we cast our cares upon the Lord, we must believe that He hears our prayers. Then we must trust God to work things out for our best interest.

God wants to partner with us to produce bumper crops in our lives that far exceed anything we've ever anticipated. If it was easy, they wouldn't call it "working" the land! Plant your dreams, your goals, then let them grow and put away your shovel!

MATTHEW 6:34
PHILIPPIANS 4:6–7
PROVERBS 16:3

WHAT NEEDS TO BE PLANTED AND GIVEN TIME TO GROW IN YOUR LIFE?

Two are better than one, because they have a good return for their labor: if either of them falls down, one can help the other up.

—Ecclesiastes 4:9–10, NIV

Firefighting is an exciting career. As a firefighter myself, two of my favorite aspects of the job are the adrenaline rush that races through your body when you hear the initial tone of the alarm, and the feeling of being part of a dedicated team. Whether we're maintaining equipment, running calls, or training, teamwork is essential. A "cowboy," in fire department lingo, is a firefighter who tends to wander off doing his own thing on a scene. Instead, he should be with his partner, performing fire ground tasks. We pair up in teams for many critical reasons, but the main priority is our safety.

Interestingly, the dictionary's definition of a cowboy is "one having qualities (as recklessness, aggressiveness, or independence)."[3] Sometimes we think we can handle life on our own. Whether our lives are smooth or we could really use some help, we must rely on God and read His word so we don't take on the cowboy mentality. God's word is our lifeline. Don't go it alone. Get involved in your local church. Hang out with your buddies. We all have similar struggles and need each other for encouragement.

Proverbs 18:24 says that *"there is a friend who sticks closer than a brother"* (NIV). Within our fire department, we have captains and firefighters who have served for over forty years. They love the camaraderie. These are leaders who impact the rest of the department with their knowledge, humor, and skill.

We need to be men who step up. Take the role of leadership and recognize the importance of surrounding yourself with reliable men who share the same beliefs and have your back. Don't be afraid to admit that you need help. Talking about personal issues will strengthen your relationships and show that you are a man of character. There's still a stigma out there that if a man admits his flaws, or drops his guard, he is weak, but in reality it's a step toward growth. Include God in your life. He wants to be part of your team, so make Him your captain!

PROVERBS 11:14
ZECHARIAH 10:5
JOHN 10:3-4

ARE YOU RELYING ON GOD OR ACTING LIKE A COWBOY?

Devotion Seven:
GET IN THE BACK SEAT!

In all your ways submit to him, and he will make your paths straight.

—Proverbs 3:6, NIV

What if one of your friends bought a new ride and tossed you the keys to go for a spin? How many of us would say that we'd rather just sit in the back? C'mon, we would drive that thing like we stole it! We want control. If he started explaining all the safety features, we might as well be wearing earplugs. Guys don't want to read the fine print. We love the look and want to know how fast we can get this thing going!

If we're not careful, we can do the same thing with God. Trying to control everything in your life causes you to have a tighter grip on your circumstance rather than helping you let go and let God. Corrie ten Boom said, "Is prayer your steering wheel or your spare tire?"[4] Wow! How true. We only let God be our backup plan. If things really get out of control, then we'll use Him.

Imagine how you would feel if you were only asked to help on-demand. God's resources are unlimited. His Word should be our steering wheel rather than our spare tire. Proverbs 3 is chock-full of blessings. Rely on God for wisdom. He promises prosperity, health, peace, protection, and a long life, among other things.

Have you ever driven in a snowstorm, or a torrential downpour? You end up gripping the wheel so tight that the tires start to slip, yet you cannot see six feet in front of your grill. The better decision would be to pull over for a breather.

The same analogy can be applied to our lives. Let God drive! You need to get in the backseat and enjoy the ride!

LUKE 9: 23–24
ISAIAH 30:21
PSALM 25:8

WHEN WAS THE LAST TIME YOU LET GOD TAKE OVER THE DRIVER'S SEAT?

Devotion Eight:
I WANT FRONT-ROW SEATS

Therefore, since we are surrounded by such a huge crowd of witnesses to the life of faith, let us strip off every weight that slows us down, especially the sin that so easily trips us up. And let us run with endurance the race God has set before us.

—HEBREWS 12:1, NLT

How many of us would jump at the chance to grab front-row seats to our favorite sports team, the Daytona 500, or concert tickets we tried to access for years? When you're watching an event on TV and see Spike Lee or Jack Nicholson sitting in VIP seats virtually next to the players, you think, "Man, just once I would love those seats." We drool over the best seats in the house. The view is perfect, the sights and sounds are magnified, you feel part of the action, and in that moment you don't even care that the credit card bill may take a year to pay off!

Do you recognize God has a front-row seat in your own life? He is your biggest fan. He loves to cheer and encourage you. He has given you skills to excel in life. Deuteronomy 28:13 says,

The Lord will make you the head, not the tail. If you pay attention to the commands of the Lord your God that I give you this day and carefully follow them, you will always be at the top, never at the bottom. (NIV)

The anticipation and excitement we feel as we wait for our event tickets is the way God feels about us. He wants us to succeed, prosper, and enjoy life. Take in all the action life has for you. Give God something to cheer about. There will always be setbacks in life, but the comebacks are worth the effort. God is a God of comebacks.

As a kid, I remember seeing an unusual guy at literally every major sporting event aired on national television. He had a wild multicolored wig and shook a John 3:16 sign. Sooner or later during the game, one of the camera crew would focus on him, drawn like a magnet! I thought to myself, "How does this guy always have front-row seats?" He was enjoying life and leaving a legacy.

Nobody's content to sit and watch a boring game, and they're disappointed when games end in a tie. Live a life that causes others to jump out of their seat cheering.

Take a few minutes today to research an amazing person named Nick Vujicic. Nick is absolutely living life in the front row, and believes his life has no limits. His faith in God has been his source of strength. Born without arms or legs, Nick overcame his disability to live a fulfilling life with a phenomenal testimony.

Mark 9:23 says that *"everything is possible for one who believes"* (NIV). Live life to the best of your ability and save a seat for God in the front row.

PSALM 139:14
COLOSSIANS 3:23
ROMANS 15:13

DO SOMETHING TODAY THAT WOULD MAKE PEOPLE STAND UP
AND CHEER LIKE A WINNING SHOT RIGHT AT THE BUZZER!

Devotion Nine:
PULL OVER

...in all your ways submit to him, and he will make your paths straight.
–Proverbs 3:6, NIV

Ever have the feeling that you're going through daily life with no real focus or direction? Has your routine each day become such a habit, way too predictable? Today may be just the time for you to refocus. Realign your priorities, and perhaps uncover or rediscover the plans God set out long ago for your life.

Each time we open our Bible, read a faith-based book, or listen to a teaching CD we receive direction for our lives. Jeremiah 29:11 says, *"For I know the plans I have for you... plans to prosper you and not to harm you, plans to give you hope and a future."* Notice that the scripture says that He *knows*. He knows our thoughts, our concerns, our hopes, and he certainly knows His plans for our lives.

Before GPS systems hit the market, we had to rely on paper maps that unfolded to the size of a small tent. If your dad was like most fathers, he would plan a family trip with a map, but sometimes he might have just packed the car till the trunk barely closed and took off!

Getting lost is an awful feeling. You become stressed, impatient, and maybe even start to argue with the other people in the car. All because you're too stubborn to pull over. As a last resort, you'll stop at a dimly lit convenience store and ask for directions at 2:23 in the morning from a guy who doesn't speak your language! By the time you admit to the crime of getting lost, you're really off-course.

God's plans are so much bigger than our own. Stay on course, follow His map, and God will lead you in the way you should be going. Twists and turns are part of life. Without them, we may miss out on opportunities we never dreamed were possible.

Be encouraged today and say out loud, "God will do amazing things in my life. I will make good decisions. I have clear direction for my future, and I believe God has a plan for my life." Relax and enjoy the journey, even if you need to pull over once in a while!

PSALM 119:59
PSALM 40:5
PROVERBS 11:14 (THE MESSAGE)
ISAIAH 30:19–21

WHERE IN YOUR LIFE DO YOU NEED GOD TO SHOW YOU THE ROADMAP?

Devotion Ten:
CONTROL THE YO-YO

These trials will show that your faith is genuine. It is being tested as fire tests and purifies gold—though your faith is far more precious than mere gold. So when your faith remains strong through many trials, it will bring you much praise and glory and honor on the day when Jesus Christ is revealed to the whole world.

—1 Peter 1:7, NLT

Have you had a recent incident in your life that felt like you got a kick in the junk? You know the feeling, like you can't catch your breath. Life can be going along smoothly when all of a sudden something hits when you least expect it. How are you going to handle this?

A red flag may be waving high in the air if your emotions are going up and down like a yo-yo on a string. One day you're up, the next day you're down, wallowing in self-pity.

Everyday our faith is going to be tested and put on display. Looking happy and thankful is easy when things are going well. Are you going to melt away when the fire comes? Make the decision to stand on the promise God has made when He says that your faith is *"being tested as fire tests and purifies gold"*? Being refined is the process of eliminated impurities.

The devil would like nothing better than to steal your joy, and create conflict and confusion in our mind. Take out some frustration on him. Let him know that none of his tricks will work on you. You have no time for yo-yo emotions, second-guessing your decisions, or feeling like you're full of flaws. Don't just build yourself up in your mind; speak it out loud and tell the devil you won't be bullied or intimidated.

James 4:7 says, *"Resist the devil, and he will flee from you"* (NLT). Take hold of the scriptures and be confident that you will not back down. Stay in control of your life. Sure, there will be days when you feel blindsided. Life may try to kick you around. But the less you yo-yo, the more you'll be able to help others overcome their challenges as they see you refined like gold!

JOSHUA 1:4–9
1 CORINTHIANS 10:13
PHILIPPIANS 4:13–14
2 TIMOTHY 1:7

IN WHAT ASPECT OF YOUR LIFE CAN GOD CAN HELP YOU CONTROL THE YO-YO?

The Lord says, "I will guide you along the best pathway for your life. I will advise you and watch over you."

—Psalm 32:8, NLT

They say we learn by repetition. Sometimes the only way to learn, as the saying goes, is by being thrown in the fire. Trials test our character.

In simulation exercises, firefighters are placed in extreme heat and heavy smoke with very little visibility, sometimes pushed to the point of becoming disorientated. We are taught to remain calm, to monitor our air, and always keep in contact with the hose line. A hose line has brass couplings with raised lugs on one side of the coupling. In extreme conditions, we are trained to feel for those lugs to determine which way to follow the hose line back out of a bad situation to safety. Our simple tagline is this: lugs lead home.

God will do the same for us. He leads and guides us, and our training is to partner with Him. Right now you may be in a financially difficult time, raising young kids, or dealing with a sickness. Whatever the situation is, at times you will feel like you're being held in the fire, and sometimes you may get burned.

Do you remember the story of Shadrach, Meshach, and Abednego, the three young men who were thrown in a fiery furnace? They refused to deny God and bow down to the golden idol. King Nebuchadnezzar was so furious that he ordered the furnace to be heated seven times hotter than normal, then have them bound with rope and thrown in the fire.

As we all know, the king later had a look in the furnace and couldn't believe his eyes. In the midst of the extreme heat and flames, the men remained unharmed. God's protection was undeniable. When they emerged, the only thing burned off were the ropes that had bound them! Talk about a line of protection!

So what will be your game plan the next time you feel like life is heating up and your faith is being tested? Remember that God is your lifeline. Stick with Him. Just like the lugs, He will lead you home.

DANIEL 3:16–30
JOHN 10:27–28
PSALM 121:7–8

SOMETIMES LIFE CAN PULL US IN ALL SORTS OF DIRECTIONS.
WHAT WILL YOU DO IN ORDER TO STAY ON THE RIGHT PATH?

...the Almighty has made my life very bitter.

—RUTH 1:20, NIV

Being positive with your words is infectious. Negativity, however, is also infectious. We are all naturally drawn to people who are uplifting, inspiring, and have an excellent outlook on life. Ask yourself, "When I'm with people, do I leave them with a positive impression?"

In the book of Ruth, there's a good story of a life filled with disappointments. Once again, God reveals His ability to provide restoration and hope. A woman named Naomi—which means "beautiful, pleasant, delightful"[5]—had a life that was far from delightful. She lost her husband and two sons and became so distraught that she changed her name to Mara, which means "bitter."[6] Basically, her life stunk. In the natural, life was bleak. Although she lost hope, God had much bigger plans in mind.

His plans are so massive in comparison to our vision. When you're in a tough time and life isn't easy, remain hopeful and speak positively about your circumstances. If we aren't careful, we can get to a point where our words stink so bad that we smell. Naomi got to a point where she blamed God verbally, yet God still turned things around for her in a very monumental way. In Ruth 1:20, Naomi says, *"[T]he Almighty has made my life very bitter."* If you can recognize her despair, you'll definitely appreciate God's restoration power!

God showed favor to Naomi and her daughter-in-law Ruth through a rich farmer named Boaz. Gleaning the barley harvest in the fields of Boaz's farm, they were able to eat and survive. Eventually, Ruth married Boaz. They had a child and Naomi became a grandmother. She helped raise her grandson, and he brought her so much joy. The latter part of Naomi's life transformed into the true definition of her name.

Is your attitude towards life going to smell so bad that even skunks run and hide? Or are you going to trust God and believe that your life will be exciting and fulfilling, with great things right around the corner?

RUTH 1–4
PSALM 139:2–3
MARK 7:20–23
PROVERBS 4:23
PSALM 1: 1–3

HAVE YOU HEARD THE SAYING, "YOU CAN ONLY SPRAY SO MUCH PERFUME ON A PIG"? DON'T BE THAT GUY NOBODY WANTS TO BE AROUND BECAUSE YOUR ATTITUDE STINKS. START THE CHANGE TODAY.

He replied, "Because you have so little faith. Truly I tell you, if you have faith as small as a mustard seed, you can say to this mountain, 'Move from here to there,' and it will move. Nothing will be impossible for you."

—MATTHEW 17:20, NIV

They say everything big starts with something small. A mustard seed is very small. If we have the faith of a mustard seed, we can move a mountain. The choice of a tiny mustard seed isn't coincidental. Neither is the significance of a mountain to describe what can be moved if we apply our faith. Our minds can grasp this visual picture in the pages of our Bible. By placing one seed in the palm of your hand, you can visualize that faith can start in small ways, then grow for God to do something significant. I understand that we would all love to see our mountains moved overnight, but be encouraged that God hears our every need, and His timing is so much better than ours!

For me, I use the analogy of a backpack. I can take it on and off over and over. As the pack becomes weighed down with worries, eventually I'll take the backpack off in frustration and say, "Here, God. I'm sorry. I continue to try and handle these things on my own." We need to put our faith and trust in Him. Don't go back to repackaging the bag all over again, continuing the same crazy cycle.

Did you know that as a young man Walt Disney was fired from his job because his boss said he didn't have enough imagination? The famous filmmaker Steven Spielberg's application to film school was denied not once, but twice, before he finally was accepted on his third try! Can you imagine the life they would have missed had it not been for their faith and belief in their dreams? Habakkuk 2:3 says, *"Though it linger, wait for it; it will certainly come and not delay"* (NIV). The scripture doesn't say *maybe*. It says it *will*.

What seed are you planting today? God's watch keeps perfect time.

MARK 11:23
JAMES 5:7-8

WHAT'S IN YOUR BACKPACK THAT MAY NEED TO BE CLEANED OUT FOR GOOD?

Give, and it will be given to you. A good measure, pressed down, shaken together and running over, will be poured into your lap. For with the measure you use, it will be measured to you.

–Luke 6:38, NIV

In 2009, a group of criminals used counterfeit debit cards to steal nine million dollars from 130 ATMs in forty-nine cities around the world, all within a time period of just thirty minutes! That's big-time fraud. Sometimes in life, things that were meant for our own good can be taken advantage of, or misused in epic proportions. These machines were developed for society's convenience. They are a privilege. Street corners, gas stations, bank entrances, cruise ships—you name the area, ATMs are everywhere. After a while, some things we have created for convenience are not appreciated.

On too many occasions in life, we look at God as an ATM machine. We're in a hurry, we leave our car running, grab our access card, punch a few numbers, and away we go. We leave once we receive. Isn't that the way we are with God? We come to Him for a need, a want, or a help. We want instant answers or solutions without the wait. Over and over we use that technique, making withdrawal after withdrawal. We want it quick and easy.

However, sooner or later we must make a deposit, or else the account runs dry. Luckily, God doesn't keep track of our withdrawals, or else we wouldn't be able to afford His bank fees.

What are you investing in? Are you a taker or a giver? Do you understand that we need to recognize God for who He is, not just what He does for us? Deposits could be made in many ways. Appreciate God by showing your thankfulness and gratitude. Be generous, give a portion of your earnings in tithe, and be an example at your work or in your community. Don't just be a taker; be a giver.

When we become too reliant on instant access, we run the risk of turning God into an impersonal experience only to get what we want. God wants us to develop a relationship with Him. If we seek Him and trust His leading, God wants to give us the desires of our heart. Patience implies enduring, or waiting without complaining. Good things come to those who wait.

Next time you go to make a withdrawal on your card, remind yourself that deposits are required, too. Instead of using God like an ATM, invest in your life with Him and receive great returns!

Cave Time Reading

PSALM 37:4
ISAIAH 65:6
MATTHEW 6:31–34
II CORINTHIANS 9:8–15

HAVE YOU BEEN FAITHFUL TO MAKE DEPOSITS TOWARDS GOD'S KINGDOM?

Devotion Fifteen:
STAND LIKE A BUCKINGHAM GUARD

Be on your guard; stand firm in the faith; be courageous; be strong.
—1 Corinthians 16:13, NIV

Other than their unusual eighteen-inch black bearskin hats, a trademark of a Buckingham Palace guard, what else comes to mind when you picture these soldiers standing at attention? Is it the uniform, their unflappable facial expression, their sense of pride in their duty? For me, they have three key traits that we can put into practice in our lives.

Stand. You will never find a guard on duty sitting down at the front gate, eating a bag of chips, because he had a rough night and doesn't feel like standing. Under no circumstances will you ever see them not standing. We need to be like guards, especially when we're weak. We can call out to God for strength to stand in all areas of our life. Standing with God will give us a better view so we can rise above our difficulties and challenges. Sometimes we need to just be quiet, stand still, and listen for God's voice.

Protect. Standing in unity, rifles at their sides, you get the impression that whatever they're protecting cannot be penetrated, and gaining access is virtually impossible. Trained to defend, their duty to protect is unshakable. Ephesians 6:11 says, *"Put on the full armor of God, so that you can take your standard against the devil's schemes"* (NIV). We have been given our own protection over the attacks we face. Each day remind yourself to declare protection over your body and mind. Life can throw all kinds of mud at you. Don't let it stick.

Be confident. For fun, how many times have you seen people try to walk up to those guards, mimic them or otherwise make those guards laugh? They don't flinch. They exude confidence. They are proud of their respected position. We need to have the same confidence in our faith. Don't be intimidated by criticism or false accusations. God has given us unlimited power, and He custom-made each one of us, so be confident.

If you're feeling tired or worn-out, be like a Buckingham guard. Stand tall, declare protection over your life and your family, be confident, and say, *"I can do all [things] through [Christ] who gives me strength"* (Philippians 4:13, NIV).

EPHESIANS 6:13–18
PSALM 46:10
ROMANS 4:20–21

ARE YOU TAKING A STAND OR SITTING DOWN ON THE JOB AS A FOLLOWER OF CHRIST?

Devotion Sixteen:
FOLLOW THE LEADER

Let your light so shine before men, that they may see your good works and glorify your Father in heaven.

—Matthew 5:16, NKJV

Jesus was a trendsetter. He was the first man to introduce us guys to the concept of a man cave. I'm sure up there were many well-worn paths along the hillside leading straight to a cave entrance where Jesus needed to get away to pray. I have no doubt that some days Jesus needed a break so badly that He kept a big stack of door tags that read: "Do not disturb. Prayer in progress." We've been following His lead ever since and have continued for the last two thousand years.

We need to run to God for direction rather than thinking we can figure things out on our own. God cares so much for us, from the minor details to the big bombs we drop on Him. Nothing comes as a surprise to God. He doesn't say, "Oh man, I didn't see that coming." Deuteronomy 31:6 of the Message Bible says that *"your God is striding ahead of you. He's right there with you. He won't let you down; he won't leave you."* Can you visualize Him running ahead, making you feel like protecting you is a high priority?

After spending time in the cave, just as mighty leaders have in the past, we too can regain our strength. When we meet with God on a consistent basis, our lives will inevitably be changed. In 1 Kings 19, Elijah took shelter and rest in a cave. In 1 Samuel 22, David ran to a cave for refuge, and over four hundred men followed his lead! John 6:15 talks about how Jesus retreated to the mountains to be alone when He recognized the people were about to make him king.

Those worn-out paths up the mountainside led to Jesus' office, where He could go to think, pray, and collect His thoughts. There is obviously a reason why men are drawn to a place to retreat from the world, to regain our strength, and for God to restore our minds. In Exodus 33, God protected Moses, telling him to hide in the cleft of a rock, covering him with His hand.

Here is an important point to remember. Sometimes we must go and wait patiently in the cleft, or our man cave, while God goes to work on our behalf. Your prayers don't need to be complicated. Just be yourself. The focus will shift from you and all your cares to following His lead, and that's when you will begin to sense His grace and find your peace.

Cave Time Reading

MATTHEW 6:6
MATTHEW 11:28–30
JUDGES 8: 1–23
DEUTERONOMY 5:33

Do you have a place where you can go to refuel?

Devotion Seventeen:
SQUASH THE BUG

Therefore, get rid of all moral filth and the evil that is so prevalent and humbly accept the word planted in you, which can save you.

—JAMES 1:21, NIV

There are lots of common bugs in this world, but some are more unusual than others. If you haven't ever heard about the boll weevil, then... well, this devotion is worth your time today. I heard about this annoying little beetle from a captivating sermon by Pastor Joel Osteen. I've learned so much from his messages over the years, and portions of this lesson are well worth repeating and can be applied to our daily life.

In a nutshell (you will realize later why I chose that word), cotton was a tremendous source of income to farmers in Alabama back in the early 1900s. Along came a small beetle that infested their fields and completely devastated not just portions, but entire crops. Cotton was an multimillion-dollar source of income, so this tiny bug was destroying their lives—and a solution was nowhere in sight, no matter how many options were tested to eliminate the pest.

Does this sound like a problem we all face in our everyday lives? Something gets a hold of us, and we can't shake it, or our whole focus revolves around the problem.

Finally, a man by the name of John Pittman recognized that in order to squash the bug, the farmers needed to diversify. The boll weevil didn't affect peanut crops. Therefore, the farmers of Enterprise, Alabama began to turn their large crops from cotton to peanuts, and within two years they were the largest peanut-producing county in the United States.

Just like our own lives, we need to recognize how something disastrous can be a catalyst for change! On our own, we sometimes cannot come up with a solution to our problems, but God can turn sour into sweet. Bon Fleming, a local businessman in Enterprise, was so grateful for the change in the local economy that he came up with the idea for "the world's only monument built to honor an agricultural pest."[7]

What is the boll weevil in your life? Ask God to help you remove that which can devastate you in order to turn your life around and unfold a great story. The monument in downtown Enterprise has been damaged and vandalized many times over the years, but nothing can take away its significance. Eliminating that bug in your life may take time and work, but it will be so worth the reward!

JOB 11:14
MATTHEW 7:4
EPHESIANS 4:31

WHAT CAN YOU DO RIGHT NOW TO SQUASH THE BUG THAT IS CREATING TROUBLE IN YOUR LIFE?

An angry person stirs up conflict, and a hot-tempered person commits many sins.

—PROVERBS 29:22, NIV

In the center of our town stands the Heinz factory, which is the world's largest ketchup-producing company. Each day at twelve o'clock sharp you can hear the long blast of a steam whistle to indicate the lunch break. A steam whistle consists of a few parts. When the lever is pulled, a valve opens to let the steam escape. Once the steam is compressed, it produces the trademark sound. Lighthouses, boats, and trains back in the day were all fitted with whistles for a warning signal or method of communication.

Anger has been referred to as a warning signal. It alerts us to those times when something or someone has pushed us beyond our boundaries. Anger becomes sin when we allow negative emotions to boil or build up pressure, like a loud steam whistle. Bottled-up emotions can even lead to sickness and health problems.

By itself, anger is not a sin; it's what we do with that anger which can lead to sin. Proverbs 29:11 says, *"Fools vent their anger, but the wise quietly hold it back"* (NLT). Try to recognize what your tipping point is. We need to learn how to vent our emotions in a way that releases the pressure before anger builds up and we lose control.

When we don't control our anger, we end up saying more than we should. We hurt people around us, and the consequences of our actions could leave deep emotional cuts that take a very long time to heal. Sometimes we say things we regret, just like squeezing a tube of toothpaste. Once it's out, it's hard to get back in!

Learn to recognize what triggers the lever in you that pressurizes emotions like a steam pipe. It has been said that learning to vent our anger to God—before unleashing it on the world—is an expression of trust. The reality is that we all have pressures in life.

Between raising kids, work demands, and other pressing concerns, we need to find ways to clear our heads. Escape to your man cave, relax, go for a run/walk, enjoy some sports, or read. Just do whatever it takes. Ask God for the strength and control to remain calm, and learn how to deal with your frustrations in a way that doesn't cause you to look like a train chugging down the tracks blowing steam into the sky!

Cave Time Reading

EPHESIANS 4:15–19
PROVERBS 15:18
JAMES 1:19–20
ECCLESIASTES 7:9

SOME GUYS HAVE A REAL PROBLEM DEALING WITH THEIR ANGER. HOW DO YOU VENT THE STEAM?

Devotion Nineteen:
DISCIPLESHIP 101: CRASH COURSE

...if you embrace this kingdom life and don't doubt God, you'll not only do minor feats... but also triumph over huge obstacles.

—MATTHEW 21:21-22

I don't know about you, but I'm not a "manual" kind a guy. If I have to put something together, I'll decide whether or not to read the manual by the number of pages it has. I would much rather learn by hands-on experience. Some people can read a book to learn, while others have to see, touch, or experience it.

Can you imagine how amazing life would have been as a disciple, spending your days under the teaching of Jesus? A day in the life with Him was frontline, one-on-one learning from the best life-skills teacher who ever walked the earth. The gospels of Matthew and Mark are full of phenomenal examples of how Jesus taught in a way no modern book could ever teach. These men watched Jesus raise people from the dead, cast out demons, and calm raging storms. By the command of His voice, the disciples saw a fig tree that was in bloom wither away in an instant and fed thousands of hungry people in one sitting, just to name a few.

Jesus was mocked by disbelieving onlookers who said He was a local boy who grew up to be just a carpenter. Just a carpenter? If that's what it looks like to be just a carpenter, then I want to be His apprentice! He was a teacher in the truest sense of the word. He got on their level.

Many times after performing miracles, the disciples had lots of questions. They would gather for a debriefing with Jesus, during which He would explain what had happened in a way they could all comprehend. Mark 4:33-34 states,

With many similar parables Jesus spoke the word to them, as much as they could understand. He did not say anything to them without using a parable. But when he was alone with his own disciples, he explained everything. (NIV)

Did He get frustrated and impatient with them regarding their lack of faith, or doubt? Absolutely! We do the same things His disciples did, yet they were walking side-by-side with Him—and they still questioned. We may not have the same opportunity as these hand-picked men who got to walk with Jesus, but the Bible teaches us how to apply these same skills and lessons. I really like how the Message Bible translates what Jesus says in Mark 6:8-9:

Don't think you need a lot of extra equipment for this. You are the equipment. No special appeals for funds. Keep it simple.

No extra tools required. No certificates. All we need are the tools He has provided for us. Every time the disciples (like us) questioned Him or had doubt or fear, it became an opportunity for Jesus to give them on-the-job training. Yes, there were times when He got upset with them, yet He did what Jesus does best: He taught.

Trade your shoes for sandals today. Take a crash course in discipleship as you read the stories in Matthew and Mark about how these men learned from the ultimate teacher.

Cave Time Reading

MARK 4:1-40

SET ASIDE SOME TIME TODAY TO THINK ABOUT WHAT YOUR SPIRITUAL GIFTS ARE.

> The men in charge of the work were diligent, and the repairs progressed under them. They rebuilt the temple of God according to its original design and reinforced it.
>
> —2 Chronicles 24:13, NIV

Take a drive around any growing city and you'll see massive cranes, scaffolding, and heavy equipment working on new projects. I'm amazed at the engineering creativity of these structures. Cities are abuzz with growth, change, and contractors who are invested in their communities.

Sometimes the rebuilding process requires a complete overhaul. Other times the builder preserves the framework, but the important factor is the integrity of the foundation. In order to rebuild, the old needs to be demolished, brought down, and cleaned up to get back to the original foundation.

I think I can write with confidence that none of us want to be torn down in our own lives, to be rebuilt. This is painful for a number of reasons. When our lives are in the renovation phase, we question why it needs to happen. We don't understand, and if we are brutally honest, it ticks us off. We're really great at being inspectors, finding faults in others, but it's a whole different ball game when we hear about our own flaws and defects.

Going through the process of being rebuilt would be so much easier if we could look beyond the work that needs to be done to see the finished product. Just like renovations, it takes time, and there may be aspects in our lives that are rotten and worn-out. Or perhaps they shouldn't have been there in the first place.

This stage can also be an exciting time, though. Not only for ourselves, but for others around us to observe the changes we've made. In a way, it's like we're having a huge yard sale, getting rid of the junk and garbage that has collected over time.

Our core foundation is the starting point. Make sure you're building on rock, not sand. The Bible says in Matthew 7:24,

Therefore everyone who hears these words of mine and puts them into practice is like a wise man who built his house on the rock. (NIV)

Just last summer, over a span of three weeks, the city of Beijing reported ninety-nine sinkhole collapses, all due to poor planning! Let's not let that happen to us. Allow God to be the architect of your life. He made the blueprint anyway! God has an incredible portfolio proving His quality workmanship.

PSALM 139:14–17
PSALM 33:11
PROVERBS 12:7

HOW DO YOU FEEL ABOUT YOUR FOUNDATION? IS IT SOLID OR IN NEED OF REPAIR?

Devotion Twenty-One:
KNOCK TILL HE BREAKS THE HINGES

Look! I stand at the door and knock. If you hear my voice and open the door, I will come in, and we will share a meal together as friends.

—Revelation 3:20, NLT

Initially my intention was to title this devotion "Knock Till You Break the Hinges"—until one night when I couldn't sleep, God spoke to me. He said, "Hey, it's not you who needs to stand at my door and knock; I'm the one who stands knocking on the door, hoping you will answer!" Ouch.

Right then, I realized it was true. God leaves out a big welcome mat at His door, and He's ready to answer our knock. It's not necessary to pound on the door, to push your nose against the glass to peer inside to see if He's home. His wish is that we make it a habit to accept His open invitation to spend time with him.

Just think about this scripture: *"we will share a meal together as friends."* It the way God loves to spend time with us, to get to know us as one would a close friend.

One day I thought to myself, "How funny that this scripture is found in Revelation." To me, being awakened to hear from God about how to revise this devotion was, in fact, a revelation. We need to understand how much He desires to be included in our lives, our decision-making, and our dreams. God isn't like the kid selling cookies at your door, or a pushy salesperson who will stand there ringing the doorbell twenty-three times until you finally answer. Sadly for us, He will knock. If we don't answer, He will patiently wait until we're ready to answer another day. I'm sure He would love to keep pounding on the door, till the hinges come loose, hoping to grab our attention, but that isn't the way God works.

John 15:5 says,

Yes, I am the vine; you are the branches. Those who remain in me, and I in them, will produce much fruit. For apart from me you can do nothing. (NLT)

I don't know about you, but I want my life to bear fruit. Accepting God into your heart and making sure you accept His invitation can only lead to you developing a close friendship and bond with the Lord. Next time you feel a knocking on your heart, recognize that God is trying to get your attention. Open the door and invite Him in.

Cave Time Reading

JEREMIAH 29:12–13
PROVERBS 16:9, NIV)
JOHN 14:23
JOHN 14:14

BIG DOORS SWING ON SMALL HINGES. WHAT DOORS ARE YOU BELIEVING GOD WILL OPEN IN YOUR LIFE?

I am the light of the world. Whoever follows me will never walk in darkness, but will have the light of life.

—John 8:12, NIV

We are blessed to live in an age of technology. Virtually any form of information is within our fingertips. We could easily lose our way on roads and highways if we didn't have access to a mobile map app or GPS.

When I think about how to apply a simplistic rule to the road of life, I would say it's important for us to tailgate the Lord. What do I mean? I mean that we can never go wrong letting the Lord lead. He would be a superior guide. He would be trustworthy. You would have confidence in His skills, and His sense of direction is impeccable. Sure, you could go out in the passing lane, put the pedal to the floor, and take your chances that you won't get busted. But you'll be uneasy the whole time, constantly scanning ahead to make sure you're going undetected, checking your mirror and looking over your shoulder. That might be fun for a while, but sooner or later you're going to get burned, and say to yourself, "That was really stupid!"

Hey, God gives us free will, and we make our own choices. He's not going to chase us around, although God sure would love if we followed His directions and obeyed His guidelines.

If you think about it, road signs are a lot like God. They're warnings to protect us and designed for our own good. They aren't made to punish us and be controlling. Signs are in place because serious accidents happen when we ignore them and think we are above the law. Signage that says "slow down," "winding road ahead," "stop," "yield," "one way," "do not enter," "sharp bend ahead," and "caution" are all applicable to living our lives for Him!

I think I would rather tailgate the Lord, follow His lead, and obey His laws than stay a crash test dummy.

PSALM 119: 33–36
PROVERBS 20:24
DEUTERONOMY 6:1–9

ARE YOU TAILGATING OR RECKLESSLY TRYING TO PUSH PAST GOD?

Devotion Twenty-Three:
EVIDENCE OF A LEGACY

...the generation of the upright will be blessed.

—Psalm 112:2, NIV

If I were to ask you who has left their fingerprints on your life, what characteristics and qualities would you say makes those people so unique? In 2012, it was estimated that the world's population was approximately seven billion. That means there are a lot of people out there from which to narrow down your choice!

Even identical twins don't have the same set of fingerprints. To me, that's a convincing piece of evidence that our God's creative designs are absolutely amazing. Just like a fingerprint confirms our identity, we can leave an impression or mark on others the way we live out our lives. People who are written or talked about long after they're gone have left a lasting legacy.

When I was young, I met a man with whom I spent a great deal of time. We did a lot of fishing and had great talks. I helped him on his family's farm, and he cut my hair for free! He had a passionate faith, loved his family, and had a weathered Bible that showed no signs of neglect.

He told me that he moved his family while they were quite young to an isolated island because God had lain it on his heart to become a pastor. This was a big sacrifice for his family, but the calling of God was evident on their lives. There he physically built a church and spiritually built up the congregation. In the winter, access to the island was difficult. Buying groceries and receiving packages via the mail plane was expensive. Since the lake was frozen over, men from the island would drive their cars twenty-six kilometers to the mainland, with planks of wood on their car roofs just in case they needed to lay them over cracks in the ice.

What lengths will we go to sacrifice for our families? He was a man who knew the significance of trusting God, of putting his faith in action. He had a burning desire for others to come to know Christ as their personal savior.

Over the years, I learned many things from him. I listened to people speak such positive words about his life, but I didn't know that he also struggled with bouts of depression. His wife told me years later that in order to fend off depression and discouragement, he would keep small handwritten notes of scripture and positive words in his shirt pocket and read them throughout the day. His roots were planted down deep and his foundation was solid.

Who was this man, you ask? The fingerprints of Philip Stahl, my grandfather, still remain all over my life. What can you do in your life to show evidence of a life well-lived?

DEUTERONOMY 6:4-9
PROVERBS 22:1
JOHN 15:5
DEUTERONOMY 7:9

ARE YOU LEAVING FINGERPRINT EVIDENCE OF A LEGACY?

Devotion Twenty-Four:
BEWARE OF THE MATADOR

Get rid of all bitterness, rage, anger, harsh words, and slander, as well as all types of evil behavior.

—Ephesians 4:31, NLT

As a little boy, I was a bit freaked out that my grandfather was missing part of his finger. Either I finally mustered up enough courage to ask him about it, or my mother explained it to me one day. When he was little, he and his brothers had the job of cutting wood for the stove. Little George was holding the block of wood while his older brother had the job of swinging the axe. His brother missed the wood one day, and from that day forward George could only count to four and a half on one hand! Talk about pain!

I mention this story because I want to express the importance of axing destructive roots in our lives. The root of bitterness can somehow, some way, weave and wrap so tight around our minds that we have to do whatever it takes to chop, burn, cut, rip, and yank it out before it consumes us. Bitterness can creep in either through circumstances or by someone who has done or said something damaging to us, and that can affect every area of our lives. Most importantly, it hinders our relationship with the Lord.

The Bible talks about this destructive root in Hebrews 12:15:

Look after each other so that none of you fails to receive the grace of God. Watch out that no poisonous root of bitterness grows up to trouble you, corrupting many. (NLT)

Rather than taking responsibility or gaining control over our own emotions, we blame God or others for the way we've gotten ourselves in a nasty, tangled mess. I understand that many situations are the result of what someone has done to us. The feelings you have are absolutely normal, and no doubt justified. However, we must ask God to help us dig that stubborn root out, whether we use an axe or an excavator!

A few years ago, I read a devotional about a vine that grows in South America. It's known as the "matador." This particular vine begins to grow at the base of a tree, slowly creeping its way up the trunk. As the vine wraps itself around the tree, it strangles the life from it. Finally, as the vine reaches the top, it produces a large flower as if to say, "Look what I have done."

Just like this matador vine kills the tree, bitterness can kill *us*. Initially a small bitterness vine or bad habit may not seem like a problem, but over time it can become an overgrown jungle. As I read about the matador, I realized the damage a bad root can cause. I had allowed a bitterness vine to grow in my heart, and now was the time to yank it out and forgive.

Many of us struggle with some form of a matador vine. Cutting down the root at the base will eliminate any opportunity to give the devil a foothold in your life. Sometimes on the surface we appear to have everything under control. However, if we dug down, what would your root system look like? Are those roots providing healthy nourishment, or is it time to let go of bitter emotions and unforgiveness? Chop that root out today, forgive the way God forgives, and choose to be better—not bitter.

Cave Time Reading

EPHESIANS 4:31
HEBREWS 12:14–17
MARK 7:20–22
1 PETER 2:1

IS THERE ANYTHING IN YOUR LIFE THAT'S IN NEED OF A GOOD PAIR OF SHEARS?

Devotion Twenty-five:
HAMMER AND SNAILS

Whatever you do, work at it with all your heart, as working for the Lord, not for human masters, since you know that you will receive an inheritance from the Lord as a reward. It is the Lord Christ you are serving.
—Colossians 3:23–24, NIV

When Henry Ford began the undertaking of the assembly line, his vision was to manufacture the most affordable, reliable vehicle through mass production. Within fifteen years of starting his company, more than half of American vehicles were black Model T Fords.

In that era, you didn't have the custom order "wish list" like we do today, with unlimited options to make your vehicle unique. The concept of a moving assembly line was unheard of. In comparison to today's standards, the line ran at a snail's pace. Ford's leadership revolutionized the auto industry. He chose to step out and into his destiny, leaving a legacy as unique as a fingerprint.

God custom-made each one of us. He isn't in the cookie-cutter business. We are made to be originals. Don't allow other people to force you into what *they* think you should do or be. We are all unique.

Society seems to elevate the status of celebrities, CEOs, and movie stars, yet everyday people make the world go around. Whether you're an electrician, plumber, factory worker, or what have you, be confident with how God made you. It has been said, "Base your self-worth on God's opinion of you." Just think about that. If you minimize your self-worth, you're criticizing Gods workmanship!

Many men of the Bible who accomplished great things were workers. Noah was a builder, Joseph was a laborer/slave for many years, Stephen was a fisherman, and Nehemiah was a bricklayer. Greatest of them all, Jesus apprenticed as a carpenter! Often we feel we like we've missed our chance, or we think that reaching the goals we set for ourselves is taking too long.

Success and fulfillment don't come overnight, but diligence leads to prosperity. Strive to become who God wants you to be, even if you're not where you want at this point. Try to stay in an attitude of faith.

In the Bible, we read that David was a man who knew how to lean on God during times of adversity. He was a man after God's own heart. Did he make mistakes? Big time! As with David, God doesn't look at the outside; He looks into your heart. Remember, it doesn't matter if you swing a hammer or are the CFO of a large firm; we all have God-given talents to use to the utmost of our ability. Whether you have attained your goals or are still making your way towards them at a snail's pace, keep moving forward!

**1 SAMUEL 16:7
ECCLESIASTES 4:4
ECCLESIASTES 6:9
1 CORINTHIANS 15:58**

WHAT TALENT DO YOU HAVE HIDDEN THAT NEEDS TO BE SHARED?

Fathers, do not provoke your children to anger by the way you treat them. Rather, bring them up with the discipline and instruction that comes from the Lord.

–EPHESIANS 6:4, NLT

How many times have you heard the saying, "He's just like his old man"? Whether good or bad, directly or indirectly, we compare, make mental notes, and judge others.

I love hockey, and so does my son. We both still play, and we love to follow the National Hockey League. Right now numerous players have made the jump from junior to pro whose fathers played in the NHL years ago. Some have skills, size, and ability much different than their fathers. Others are definitely "just like the old man." I like spending time talking to my son about these players and which of their fathers' qualities I see in them.

We all have opportunities as fathers, grandfathers, and future dads to bond with our sons and show them how to live a life that is Christ-centered. There are going to be days when you feel really great about your skills as a dad, and then there are going to be some when you tank! Keep trying. Keep praying for wisdom. Recognize that your son is watching how you handle the good, the bad, and the ugly situations.

Some of you may say, "Well, I had a lousy father," or "I grew up in a home with an absent dad," or "Mine was too busy to make time for me." Hopefully you see the importance of breaking that cycle, and are trying to draw from other positive role models in your life. God sees your effort and will reward you.

As a father, you may not always get the "most popular dad" trophy, but now more than ever fathers need to step up and take ownership in the lives of their kids. Proverbs 22:6 says, *"Train up a child in the way he should go, and when he is old he will not depart from it"* (NKJV).

I don't know about you, but I sure want to be known for my fathers' good qualities when people say, "He's just like his old man."

- Recognize that being a father is a privilege and a gift.
- Lead by example. Be encouraging, supportive, and make them a priority.
- Celebrate their accomplishments, big and small.
- Be a teacher, not a drill sergeant (Proverbs 22:6).
- Don't coddle them; they are going to make mistakes.
- Be a good listener.
- Be strong enough to talk about uncomfortable things.
- Don't be a know-it-all; they will quit asking.
- Keep trying, even if you mess up (Isaiah 40:30–31).
- Show them how to respect and treat women.
- Be generous, volunteer, and let them see you helping others in need.
- Live what you believe (Proverbs 16:23).
- Make them feel important.
- Going to work isn't the only way to be a provider; teenagers want your dime, but they also need your time!
- Watch your words (James 3:7–13).

Take a few minutes this week in your man cave to check out these amazing dads:

- Patrick John and Patrick Henry Hughes: http://www.youtube.com/watch?v=-qTiYA1WiY8
- Rick and Dick Hoyt: http://www.youtube.com/watch?v=64A_AJjj8M4

If you're a dad, when was the last time you had a quality talk with your child?

Devotion Twenty-Seven:
GET ON BASE

And without faith it is impossible to please God, because anyone who comes to him must believe that he exists and that he rewards those who earnestly seek him.

—HEBREWS 11:6, NIV

With today's technology, we can access virtually any information instantly. Grab your phone, tap a few buttons, and you have internet, news updates, banking, email, and unlimited apps. The negative part to this is that the world has taught us that we can demand immediate results. We become impatient and try to eliminate the parts between start and finish. We want to go from the batter's box to home plate with one crack of the bat!

Ted Williams, a famous baseball player, began his career and finished it with the same team, the Boston Red Sox. He once said, "A man has to have goals—for a day, for a lifetime—and that was mine, to have people say, 'There goes Ted Williams, the greatest hitter who ever lived.'"[8] During his career, he reached base an astounding forty-eight percent of the time. Williams also had a .553 on-base percentage that stood as a record for sixty-one years! He knew that getting on base was just as important as hitting home runs. Williams won the American League batting title six times despite missing five years to military service in World War II and the Korean War.

We, too, can have setbacks in our lives and careers, but the key is to keep swinging. The learning curve is truly when we grow as people. We gain skills, become reliable in adversity, and develop patience. There will be days when we get into a slump. Keep your focus on God and remind yourself that God is a rewarder *of "those who earnestly seek him"* (Hebrews 11:6, NIV). We don't always have to swing for the fences. We just need to get on base.

I believe God writes down the times when we take small steps, that He is proud of our faith. We must step out, believing that He knows we may sometimes feel stuck in our daily grind, a struggling marriage, or a difficult circumstance. We pray the quick-fix prayer, asking God to take our problems away... now! Sometimes He does, but more often we see our biggest growth when He doesn't provide the quick fix. Faith is then activated and we make progress.

Ted Williams decided to retire in 1960 after an illustrious career. In his last game, on his final turn at bat, Williams stepped up to the plate and cranked a home run! He wanted folks to say he was the greatest hitter of all time. When you walk down the street, what do you want folks to say about you? Are you leaving a lasting impression?

Whatever season you're in, stay patient, and keep taking small steps towards your goals. Soon those singles and doubles will turn into the home run you've been waiting for!

Cave Time Reading

JAMES 2:20
1 PETER 4:10-14
MATTHEW 25:21-23

HOW CAN YOU MAKE A POSITIVE, GODLY INFLUENCE ON THIS WORLD?

Devotion Twenty-Eight:
SIX-PACK

I discipline my body like an athlete, training it to do what it should.
—1 CORINTHIANS 9:27, NLT

If you grab a magazine off the shelf about men's health or fitness, you won't see a fat guy eating a donut lounging in his favorite chair. Normally, you'll see some dude with a six-pack, or an article about the latest quick-fix technique to improve your core. I'm all for healthy living and staying in shape, but it takes work. Getting a six-pack takes a *lot* of work!

Your core is referred to as the central, innermost part. Staying physically fit is important. Conditioning and maintaining your inner core is vital. The effort and devotion you put into your training applies to both your physical and spiritual body. You need to fill the tank with the word of God so your core is firm and solid.

The Bible is full of incredibly uplifting stories, encouragement, direction, discipline, and guidance. There's a ton of excellent resource books available, but not one compares to the unlimited resources available to us in the Bible.

Strengthening your core by staying physically fit requires commitment, dedication, and making time to work out a priority in your busy lifestyle. When we're not physically active, we become lethargic. We lack energy. Sometimes we give up, feeling like we've gone so far from where we want to be that hope is stuck deep in the couch cushion.

The same goes for us spiritually. Being a "Chreaster" (going to church at Christmas and Easter), doing the occasional devotion, or saying the "Help me, God" prayer won't cut it for staying spiritually fit.

The Message Bible says,

Everyone runs; one wins. Run to win. All good athletes train hard. They do it for a gold medal that tarnishes and fades. You're after one that's gold eternally. (1 CORINTHIANS 9:24)

Make God a priority in your life. Set aside time each day to keep your inner core fit. Just like staying active, develop a daily routine of spending time with God. Run your race, give it everything you've got, and keep working on that spiritual core!

ISAIAH 40:29–31
2 CORINTHIANS 4:16
DEUTERONOMY 34:7

WHAT STEPS ARE YOU TAKING TOWARDS SPIRITUAL FITNESS?

> Woe to you, teachers of the law and Pharisees, you hypocrites! You clean the outside of the cup and dish, but inside they are full of greed and self-indulgence. Blind Pharisee! First clean the inside of the cup and dish, and then the outside also will be clean.
>
> —Matthew 23:25–26, NIV

Okay, so the title may sound harsh, but sometimes there's no other way to describe what some people are like, right? Let's be honest. Some people have nothing good to say. They bring us down, and they suck the life right out of us. Or worse yet, what if you have a reputation for being the guy who claims to have a relationship with God, but your lifestyle is far from lining up with who you really are in Christ? Such a person might be rolled in icing sugar, but he's still a turd!

If we see this in ourselves or others, what do we do? How do we handle our emotions when these types of people come in and out of our lives? Difficult people test our faith. "Turning the other cheek," as the Bible tells us to do, isn't so easy when they're right in our faces, spewing verbal diarrhea! If we aren't careful, we won't be able to contain our emotions, and we'll end up saying or doing something we could regret.

Someone gave me a great piece of advice and said, "Don't take the bait!" That is a simple and true statement. We have the power of choice. We can get sucked into taking the bait, or we can control our mouths. Being a spirit-filled believer of Christ doesn't make you a doormat, but you need to constantly be aware of your words and the choice to respond or just let something go.

Proverbs 13:3 reads, *"Those who guard their lips guard their lives, but those who speak rashly will come to ruin"* (NIV). Or how about this, in James 3:8: *"But no one can tame the tongue. It is a restless evil, full of deadly poison"* (NLT). The Bible is full of flashing warning signs to keep a short leash on our tongues.

Sometimes people will seem to make it their mission to find fault in every aspect of our lives. Make the decision to not take the bait. Cast that care to God and remain at peace. When you choose to stay in control, it will show that you have discipline. Just remind yourself: they might roll themselves in sugar, but they're still a turd... and that really stinks!

Cave Time Reading

MARK 7:9–23
MATTHEW 7:15
MARK 12:34–37
PSALM 19:14
PROVERBS 16:24
PROVERBS 25:26

DOES YOUR EXTERIOR MATCH UP WITH WHAT'S UNDER THE HOOD?

Devotion Thirty:
FRIENDS–CHOOSE A PAUL, NOT A SAUL

There are "friends" who destroy each other, but a real friend sticks closer than a brother.

–PROVERBS 18:24, NLT

Who we choose to spend time with can affect all aspects of our lives. We can be encouraged, inspired, and challenged by our choice of friends. We can be lifted up–or dragged down, if we're not careful. After spending time hanging out with a friend, do you walk away feeling good, or do you feel like a wet rag that's been wrung out from all the drama and turmoil in their life?

Take a few minutes today to compare the lives of King Saul and Paul and determine who you would prefer to build a friendship with. Interestingly, God had very big plans in place for them, yet both started off in polar opposite places. They finished their lives making a complete reversal from the way they started, as if they intersected and changed positions. Sadly, one chose to walk with the Lord while the other walked away.

- Saul was a king who lost his crown due to sin. Paul was full of sin, then was radically changed and became an apostle who received a crown.
- God confronted Saul, later named Paul, in a miraculous way by knocking him off his horse. Saul needed to get knocked off his horse!
- Paul tried to build up and encourage his successor, Timothy. Saul tried to kill his successor, David, numerous times out of jealousy.

- Paul's life and name changed when h dropped his pride and picked up humility. Humility faded from Saul's life; he got a big ego and picked up a bushel full of pride.
- Paul received his position because of obedience. King Saul lost his position because of disobedience.
- Paul was not a jealous man; King Saul was an extremely jealous man.
- Paul had people's backs, but with Saul you had to watch your back!
- Paul had clarity. Saul had confusion.
- Both men died fighting... King Saul due to sin and Paul due to his passion to save sinners.

So which one would you choose? I would say it's a no-brainer. I want to be an example to my friends that I can enjoy life, have fun, and live a life that's pleasing to the Lord. Even if you feel like Paul, who didn't start his life walking on the right side, you can make the change and takes steps towards a brighter future!

1 CORINTHIANS 15:33
PROVERBS 22:25

ARE YOU HANGING OUT WITH SAULS OR PAULS?

Like cold water to a weary soul is good news from a distant land.

—PROVERBS 25:25, NIV

Our minds soak up our emotions and experiences. Some we soak in, and some we just need to wring out! A sponge has the ability to absorb water, while our minds are known for their amazing ability to retain a tremendous amount of information. A dry sponge is useless until you soak it. When you add water, it gets trapped inside all the empty spaces until the sponge is forcibly squeezed out.

When we saturate our minds with God's word, and positive thoughts, we'll be able to work like a sponge by forcibly squeezing out the garbage and negativity, making room for more positive, helpful information.

Science says that water molecules like to stick to, or attract, one another. As we strengthen our relationship with Christ, the things we continue to learn will stick to what we already have stored in our minds until we have a heavy, spiritually full sponge.

Past disappointments and mistakes may be hard to erase or wipe out of our memory if we hang on to them for the wrong reasons. Going through difficult situations can actually make us stronger, and help us avoid repetitive mistakes in the future.

I truly believe we all have a story and testimony from the things we've stored away. You don't get a testimony without tests. Be open for opportunities to talk about your faith, and provide some water to someone who feels they're completely dried up.

What have you allowed to soak in your life that could be exactly what someone else needs to hear? What experience have you gone through that needs to be told?

Make the most of your opportunities to pass on what you've learned and experienced when the opportunity arises. Remember: *you* may be the only Bible they ever read!

JEREMIAH 31:25
PHILIPPIANS 4:8

Is there someone you know who could use your help this week?

So do not throw away this confident trust in the Lord. Remember the great reward it brings you!

—Hebrews 10:35, NLT

Although I have never been on a sailboat, I can see the importance of having wind. As the wind comes from behind, you open the sails as far as they will go so the wind pushes against them and carries the boat along the water. Rather than fighting the wind, you must work with it to receive the benefit of the power.

Do you ever feel like you're fighting the wind during certain circumstances in your life? Life can roll along so much better if you learn how to change your attitude and take advantage of the winds of our day-to-day lives rather than making it a constant battle. There is a drastic visual difference when you picture a boat struggling to fight against the wind and another boat sailing along as the wind does the work.

In the book of Acts, there is a story played out in the life of Paul. Along with over 250 men, Paul was a prisoner on a ship that got caught in rough, treacherous seas for days on end. The wind was relentless, the waves pounded the boat, and the men became weaker by the day. In order to stay afloat and lighten the ship's weight, they threw anything not required overboard, including their food. As the ship continued to be driven off-course, the men started to lose hope. Death at sea loomed.

Paul was the only man on that ship who was promised to survive. In God's perfect timing, an angel appeared to him confirming everyone's safety. He told this to the men and restored their hope. Acts 27:22 says, *"But now I urge you to keep up your courage, because not one of you will be lost"* (NIV). By expressing his confidence in God, the others on the ship respected Paul and trusted him—and saving the lives of these men gave Paul credibility to talk to them about eternal life later on.

Storms of life can really overwhelm us. Rather than losing hope and trying to save ourselves on our own strength, we need to rely on the one who assures us He can calm our storms. We can be an example to others about how to ride out our storms and not only survive, but thrive. Paul didn't throw away his confidence, and neither should we!

Cave Time Reading

DANIEL 11:32
PSALM 19:14
PROVERBS 16:24

SOONER OR LATER, A STORM OF LIFE WILL COME UP. HOW CAN YOU PREPARE YOURSELF SO YOU'LL HAVE THE SPIRITUAL STRENGTH TO WEATHER THE STORM?

Devotion Thirty-Three: CAMPING WITH JEREMY

Live wisely among those who are not believers, and make the most of every opportunity. Let your conversation be gracious and attractive so that you will have the right response for everyone.

—Colossians 4:5–6, NLT

Camping is a great way to spend time with friends and family. We reconnect. We escape from everyday routines to take a break hanging out, listening to stories, and making memories. By slowing down our pace, we take advantage of opportunities we would have missed in our fast-paced lifestyles.

The way God sets up circumstances and situations is not coincidental. Stay open for your moment to be used by God. Someone will come across your path who needs to hear your story, or they'll have exactly what you've been seeking for encouragement during a difficult time. The key is to be patient and remain at peace while you're at "camp," waiting for your breakthrough.

In the book *I Still Believe*, by Jeremy Camp,[9] there's an extraordinary example of making the most of an opportunity when God plays director. After an extremely difficult series of events in Jeremy's life, God placed a homeless man named David directly in his path. Due to David's drug and alcohol addiction, his marriage broke down and he was living on the streets. With Jeremy's mind on his own issues, he quickly walked by David with only a slight acknowledgement.

After a few minutes, Jeremy felt bad and asked the Lord to give him another opportunity to speak to David. Within a few minutes, and to his amazement, Jeremy saw

David sitting outside a restaurant. They went in, had some burgers, and talked about their lives. After hearing about David's hardships, he asked Jeremy what his job was.

"I play Christian music," Jeremy said.

David replied, 'Is your last name Camp?"

Only months before, a friend had given David a copy of Jeremy's CD! God can cause our lives to intersect in the most unpredictable ways. When the Holy Spirit prompts you to reach out, be obedient. Take time to camp with God. Share your story.

You cannot imagine the power and impact that can be made through your openness to give or receive encouragement.

Just before they went their separate ways, Jeremy felt strongly that he should encourage David. "God's going to restore your marriage," Jeremy said. "He brought me into your life for a reason."

About eight years after their meeting, Jeremy received an email from a woman asking if he remembered David. She wanted to let him know that David was clean and God had completely restored their marriage. Wow!

Remember: when you go through rough circumstances, God just might be at work turning a negative situation into a powerful testimony that will impact the lives of many people and leave you amazed at His goodness.

ROMANS 5:1–21
PHILIPPIANS 2:4
2 CORINTHIANS 3:18

JEREMY WAS OPEN TO GOD SPEAKING TO HIM. TAKE SOME TIME TO CAMP
WITH GOD AND HEAR WHAT HE HAS TO SAY TO *YOU*.

Devotion Thirty-Four:
JESUS WEARS JEANS

Then call on me when you are in trouble, and I will rescue you, and you will give me glory.

—Psalm 50:15, NLT

Remedy Drive, a Christian band, has a song called "Speak to Me." It talks about one's desire to hear from God. When you hear the chorus, you can hear their desire and desperation for God to speak to them. I want to hear directly from the Lord so clearly like men did in the Bible. Men like Moses, David, Elisha, Gideon, and Paul.

When I was really discouraged one day, I took a long ride on the negative train. I headed home for lunch, letting God know how defeated I felt. As I walked up the stairs and opened the front door, I felt as if Jesus was casually leaning against the wall, hands behind His back, wearing a pair of jeans. I would describe His face as having a look that said He was fed up with my attitude. It seemed so vivid, as if He was standing by the cupboard filled with books and pointed to the shelf to say, "Come over here, open your devotional to page 81, and read it!"

I had no doubt in my mind that He was directing me to *exactly* the page I needed to read. When I read that page, I was astounded. The words were truly what I had been concerned about, and it gave me scripture to confirm how to handle it.

Sometimes we get desperate to hear from the Lord. He can whisper or shout, it really doesn't matter. We just need to close our mouths, stop giving God our wish list, and open our eyes and ears for the answers He will provide.

Some of you have felt the same way and can relate to this. Yet others may think this is a bit strange. I share my personal experiences because they left such an impact on me that I hope these words will encourage you. Psalm 55:22 says, *"Give your burdens to the Lord, and he will take care of you. He will not permit the godly to slip and fall"* (NLT).

There are days when we feel like our heads are in a fog and we cannot see past where we are at right now. God's word tells us that He knows the number of hairs on our heads. He cares enough about each one of us that He can direct you to the very page of a devotional that provides just what you need to hear!

PSALMS 139:23
JAMES 5:13–16
PSALMS 18:6

WOULD GOD NEED TO SHOUT IN ORDER TO GET YOUR ATTENTION AT THIS STAGE OF YOUR LIFE?

Devotion Thirty-Five:
NUTS, BOLTS, AND SCREW-UPS...

Thank you for making me so wonderfully complex! Your workmanship is marvelous—how well I know it.

—Psalm 139:14, NLT

How do you feel after you've overcome a challenge or fear? Do you feel a sense of relief, a feeling of completion, or a rush of energy? Trying to be a better man, husband, or father by stretching beyond our comfort zone takes effort and energy.

When I was young, I absolutely dreaded the thought of having to go in front of my classmates to present a topic for public speaking. Even today, I haven't overcome the feeling of being uncomfortable and nervous. I still think that I'm going to screw up.

We have the choice to avoid our fears at all costs and not even try. Or we can accept the challenge. Ask God for His strength and help, and use the opportunity to improve in the areas of your life where you lack confidence. Don't beat yourself up! God has a plan for you.

Jeremiah 29:11 says,

For I know the plans I have for you... plans to prosper you and not to harm you, plans to give you hope and a future. (NIV)

You really never know what God has in store for your life or what's behind the curtain if you don't push through your feelings of discomfort, fear, or failure.

Have you heard the saying that goes, "Sometimes you gotta get pushed out of your nest in order to learn to fly"? When a mother eagle decides her baby is ready to fly, she pushes the bird out of the nest. It will flip and flop in the air as it learns how to fly. During the process, it will at times look like it's going to crash-land, but at the last moment the mother will swoop down and catch the baby, carry it back up to the nest, and start the process again until it learns to fly on its own.

Maybe you haven't yet figured out the gifting God has blessed you with, or you're frustrated waiting to find the sweet spot in your life. Perhaps fear has gripped you so tight that you've lost your desire to seek your dreams. Just remember that no matter how young or old you are, it's never too late. Continue to ask God for direction, tighten up those nuts and bolts that hold you together, and pursue with confidence the abilities and talents God has placed within you.

PSALM 31:3
PSALM 143:8
1 PETER 4:10
PHILIPPIANS 4:6–7

IS THERE A SPIRITUAL GIFT THAT NEEDS TO BE UNCOVERED IN YOUR LIFE?

The remaining five devotions are based on paintings I have completed over the last few years. For me, spending time in my cave is a way to think about the direction my life is going, slow down, and ask God for help in all areas.

One thing that really helped clear my head was rekindling my passion to create art. In a way, it became a form of therapy. As you read these final devotionals, I hope you'll see how God was dealing with me and providing an outlet.

Over the next few pages, perhaps there's something you've been kicking around for a long time that you want to pursue, change, or break free from as you spend time in your cave...

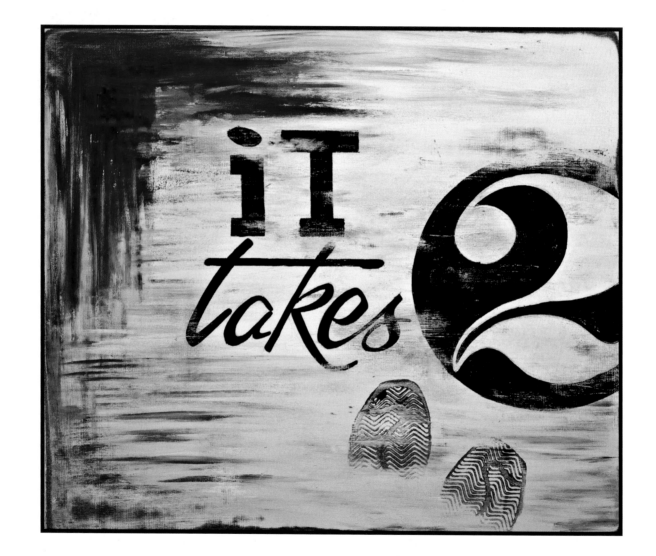

Devotion Thirty-Six:
IT TAKES TWO

The Lord directs our steps, so why try to understand everything along the way?

—Proverbs 20:24, NLT

What's the first thought that pops into your head regarding the words "it takes two"? Matthew 14 talks about Jesus walking on water. Initially when the disciples saw Him approach their boat, walking across the rough, choppy water, they thought they had seen a ghost and were terrified. Jesus spoke to them and said, "Take courage. It is I. Do not be afraid." In reply, Peter said, "Lord, if it's you, tell me to come to you on the water." Peter was willing to take that risk.

In the natural, walking on water would be a ridiculous decision, yet he stepped out of the boat. As long as he kept his eyes on Jesus, Peter didn't doubt or fear. For me personally, stepping out with one foot is an acceptable risk. I may be hesitant. I may question my decision, or play the what-if game, but adding a second foot and fully committing is a massive step of faith.

Life provides continual challenges and rough waters. Many of us would rather cling to the safety of our comfort zone. I knew in my heart for a very long time that I was discontented, and I wasn't sure how to control my fears. I constantly questioned my decisions and skills rather than accepting new steps as an essential learning process.

In my life, the words "it takes two" signifies a number of meanings. It takes two people to argue or fight, it takes two feet to move forward, and it takes two to make a relationship work. Sadly, I harbored my emotions and didn't take too many big steps for fear of failure.

I now see how God will encourage us as we move forward and take our eyes off our feet, and focus on Him. Do not allow fear to stifle your creativity and happiness. As you step out, expect God to meet you, and watch the exciting things that come from your faith. This can be confusing. How do you know when to step out in faith and when you're supposed to sit back patiently and let God lead?

For a few years now, God has been working on me to step out with both feet, and I know He won't let me go under.

Painting the "it takes two" art was definitely God-inspired. It has been a motivating reminder for me in so many ways, and I believe it will for you, too! In what area of your life is God asking you to step out with both feet, just like the soles of my shoes on the print? As Max Lucado wrote, "If there were a thousand steps between us and God, He will take all but one. He will leave the final one to us. The choice is ours."[10]

MATTHEW 14:22-33
JEREMIAH 29:13
1 SAMUEL 17:33-37

WHAT AREA IN YOUR LIFE DO YOU NEED GOD TO GIVE YOU
THE COURAGE TO STEP OUT WITH BOTH FEET?

Devotion Thirty-Seven:
ART ACHE

A happy heart makes the face cheerful, but heartache crushes the spirit.
                                                            —PROVERBS 15:13, NIV

I named this drawing "Art Ache" after I completed it. For me, the art expresses the way I was feeling at the time. I knew God had a plan for my life. I wasn't letting go of my commitment to Him, yet I had heartache for a number of reasons. I sketched the heart wrapped in a whole mess of tangled lines because sometimes life and circumstances just keep weaving around, binding us up. Thankfully, with God we can cut ourselves loose.

I think there is a real significance in the simplicity of a heart with a band aid patch to express protection and covering over a wound. Slapping a band aid on a deep cut definitely helps protect a wound, but time is what we need for the healing process to work.

Remember when you were a kid jumping that huge ramp you made with your buddies out of junky wood scraps? You had a blast until you or your friend wiped out and ended up with a nasty cut full of gravel! Wounds really hurt, and they take a long time to heal. Do you also remember trying to act cool, as if it didn't hurt because some older guys—or even worse, a cute girl—watched as you lost control in midflight?

From boys to grown men, we tend to hide our feelings. We think we need to maintain our composure and try not to show signs of weakness. For some reason, we feel the need to just stick a band aid over our issues and hope the pain goes away.

I am so grateful that God and His word can teach us how to handle our troubles or hurts when we feel like we've been punched in the gut. Psalm 34:18 says, *"The Lord is close to the brokenhearted; he rescues those whose spirits are crushed"* (NLT).

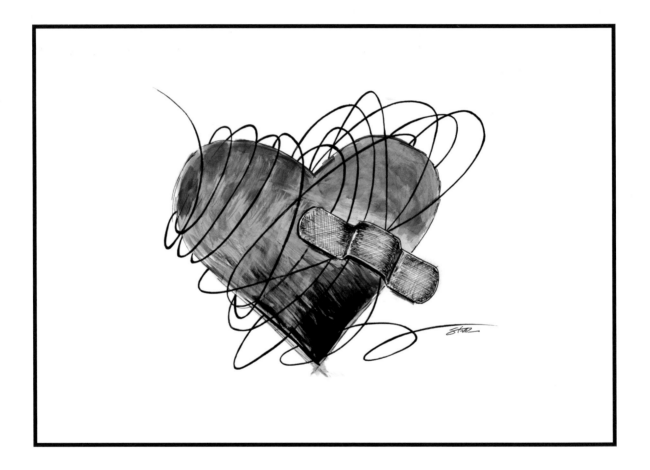

Thankfully, over time the hurts heal up and the tests we endured prove to us that we have the strength through Christ to dust ourselves off and carry on.

Remind yourself by saying, "God, I believe you are going to take these tests I've gone through and give me a testimony." We would all love to avoid hurts and pain, although that's not reality. Boxers don't enter the ring with the mentality that they're going to lose. To win the fight, they have to take some punches and battle through the pain. Show the devil that you may have been down, but you're definitely not out!

Cave Time Reading

JOB 11:13-19
PSALM 147:2-6
PSALM 73:25-28
1 PETER 3:13-16

HAVE YOU BEEN REAPPLYING A BAND AID TO THE SAME CUT?

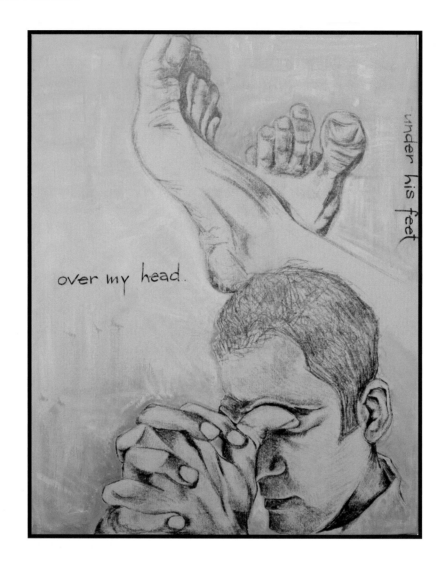

Devotion Thirty-Eight:
OVER MY HEAD, UNDER HIS FEET

And God placed all things under his feet and appointed him to be head over everything for the church, which is his body, the fullness of him who fills everything in every way.

–Ephesians 1:22–23, NIV

When people say that something is over their head, they normally mean that the subject is way beyond their control or they don't understand what's going on. When I say "under His feet," I mean that our problems are under the feet of Jesus. We acknowledge that there's peace being sandwiched in the middle, knowing we cannot control certain circumstances, yet we're under God's protection. Finding that place can be a relief. This piece of art had God's fingerprints all over the canvas.

One night when I didn't have much going on, I started sketching away with no real visual of how I wanted the finished product to look, but I knew I wanted to include those words. For some reason, I kept thinking about my daughter, and I'm sure I was saying a few prayers for her. Raising teenagers can cause any parent to take many rides on the emotional roller coaster. They know we love them, but some days parents fall below the radar on their kids' priority list, and trying to keep guidelines for them to follow will never win us any popularity contests!

As I finished the painting, I received a phone call that my daughter had to call the police on her boyfriend because there had been a physical altercation. After an emotional night, the following day I said to her, "You aren't going to believe what I painted last night." At the exact moment this issue was happening, God had placed her on my mind while working on the art piece.

The next day, when I showed her the art, we were both amazed at how God places people on our hearts during difficult times. Sometimes we don't understand why we do the things we do, or why certain things happen. Eventually situations become clear, the fog lifts, and we see how God has had His hands on our lives all along. We must keep the lines of communication open with Him.

Even though that night was a traumatic experience, I felt peace. I know with assurance, and have seen firsthand, that even if life goes over our head, it will remain under His feet!

PSALM 121:5–8
PHILIPPIANS 4:6
PSALM 8:6

CAN YOU THINK OF A SITUATION OR CIRCUMSTANCE
THAT YOU NEED TO PLACE UNDER GOD'S FEET?

Devotion Thirty-Nine: RELAX

Are you tired? Worn out? Burned out on religion? Come to me. Get away with me and you'll recover your life. I'll show you how to take a real rest. Walk with me and work with me—watch how I do it. Learn the unforced rhythms of grace. I won't lay anything heavy or ill-fitting on you. Keep company with me and you'll learn to live freely and lightly.

–Matthew 11:28-29

S ydney J. Harris once wrote, "The time to relax is when you don't have time for it!"[11] That saying is so true. Why do we get so busy? Our calendars need calendars! If we don't have the latest cell phone or electronic gadget to keep us up to speed, we feel like technology is going to leave us in the dust. We text our kids from room to room rather than walk twelve steps, and they text us at the dinner table to pass the potatoes while they check their Twitter, Instagram, and email accounts!

Learning to relax is a work in progress. We tend to create busy lifestyles by the choices we make. We work longer hours, have two or more jobs, have kids who are involved in nineteen activities, and have bigger homes but spend less time in them. We've become so accustomed to this lifestyle that we're not sure how to pull back on the reins.

How do we focus on the life we want without stopping to figure out what we're looking for? Prioritize. Make time each day for God. If it requires you to designate a set time with an alarm, then do so. How good does a cold glass of water taste if you've worked in the scorching sun all day without taking a break? The same goes for our

spiritual health. A few minutes set aside each day to read a devotional or some scripture in the Bible is just as refreshing.

Consistency is the key. Find ways to relax. Some of us read, listen to music, go outdoors, play sports, volunteer, or do other activities that recharge our batteries. For me, one way to relax is art. Most of the art I've done in the last three years incorporates words. I have a desire to create art that comes from within. I realize there's a common theme that runs through most of my pieces. Clearly, I was worn out at one time. Emotionally, I was running on fumes. It was healing to take time to relax my mind and find a quiet place to talk to God while I painted.

The famous author A.A. Milne has been quoted as saying, "Sometimes I sits and thinks and sometimes I just sits."[12] Maybe it is time for you to "just sits" and relax in God's presence and thank Him for all his blessings in your life!

Cave Time Reading

PSALM 9:9–10
ISAIAH 40:31
HEBREWS 13:6

WRITE DOWN AT LEAST THREE ACTIVITIES THAT HELP YOU RELAX AND PREVENT THE HAMSTER-IN-THE-WHEEL LIFE WE ALL FIND OURSELVES LIVING SOME DAYS.

Devotion Forty:
I AM FREE!

I will walk in freedom, for I have devoted myself to your commandments.
—Psalm 119:45, NLT

To celebrate the grand opening of a new Chinese restaurant in our city this past week, the owner had a one-day-only open invitation to enjoy a buffet meal absolutely free! What a generous offer! People were lined up out the door and around the building all day long. Sadly, the waitresses caught a few people sneaking in containers so they could bring "a little extra" home with them! Come on. Really, people? Talk about taking advantage of a gift.

People do some ridiculous things for the sake of getting something for free. They'll risk losing a limb from frostbite waiting all night for a free door-crasher giveaway, or stand in a line for an hour to eat at a free buffet till they need to be wheeled out. Are we just as eager to volunteer our free time, or are we going to say we're just "too busy"?

As I thought about what to write regarding the "I Am Free" art piece, I tried to go back and think about why those words came to my mind. Was God reminding me to quit trying to figure things out on my own understanding? We definitely gain a sense of freedom when we apply scripture to our life, such as Matthew 6:27—*"Can any one of you by worrying add a single hour to your life?"* (NIV) No, we cannot.

When I created this art, I was drawing closer to the Lord and adjusting my life by rekindling friendships, connecting more with family, pursuing peace, and regaining my self- worth. Seeking God and asking for direction in life doesn't cost us a thing. We won't receive a bill in the mail or counselling session fee for God's services. God is available like a twenty-four-hour emergency call centre. I wouldn't say we purposely set out to take advantage of Him, but sometimes we may take God for granted and forget to be grateful for the good things in our lives. God wants us to be set free from whatever is keeping us in chains.

There are numerous issues we may struggle with, yet change starts with one person: you! Make the choice to get free. Grab a pen and start to form a list of the positive things in your life. Break away from negative thoughts.

Initially when I finished this piece, I only had the word "free." After a couple weeks, I went back and added the "I am." Maybe I was beginning to feel stronger emotionally, or perhaps it was a step of faith to becoming more spiritually healthy. Either way, I pray that as you've read these devotions God has been working on your heart as He has with mine, so we can all get free.

ROMANS 6:14
JAMES 1:25
JOHN 8:34–36
PSALM 91:14–15

THE NEXT TIME YOU GET SOMETHING FOR FREE, REMEMBER THAT THIS IS HOW GOD WANTS YOU TO LIVE!

Wrap Up / Curtain Call!

They say that if you're consistent with something for a period of twenty-one days, give or take, it will become a habit in your life. For that reason, I doubled the amount of devotions within these pages, just to make sure you get committed and won't leave me stuck in the cave alone!

I hope after reading these forty devotions that you've recognized how vital it is to spend daily time with God and read His word. It can change your life. I encourage you to grasp ahold of another devotional and continue to make this part of your daily routine. There are numerous excellent resources out there to provide encouragement, life lessons, and powerful scripture to keep you consistently wanting to spend time in your cave, wherever that place may be.

As you read this book, I pray something in your heart was stirred up, and that you have done a diagnostic check around yourself regarding your progress. Have you found areas that require some repair? Trust me, I've been there and continue to be each day.

There are going to be times when you feel as though you've completely ran out of gas and there's nothing left in the tank. Learn from your flaws and celebrate your successes. God sees your potential.

The first scene in the movie *The Lucky One* (sorry, it's a bit of a chick flick) begins with a fishing boat travelling down a calm, winding river as the narrator provides these words:

You know, the smallest thing can change a life. In the blink of an eye, something happens by chance—and when you least expect it—since we're on a course that you could have never planned, into a future you never imagined. Where will it take you? That's the journey of our lives: our search for the light. But sometimes, finding the light means you must past through the deepest darkness.[13]

I think this is a fantastic quote. If I could change just one word, I would replace "chance" and insert "God." I do believe we all go through times in our lives, as we're searching for the light, that we must pass through our deepest darkness. I believe this is why I feel so compelled to ask the question, "Where is your man cave?" We all need a place to go to regain our strength, retreat, relax, and to seek encouragement and direction from the Lord.

One of my all-time favorite stories in the Bible is a passage found in 1 Samuel 30. The message in this story impacted my life so much that I'm forever stamped with a tattoo design based on the strength of David digging deep and rallying his troops to victory. 1 Samuel 30:6 says, *"But David found strength in the Lord his God"* (NIV). David and his army got themselves to a point of complete distress both mentally and physically, yet David knew he was able to strengthen himself in the Lord. Why? He had a personal relationship with the Lord Jesus Christ. Just like David, we must strengthen ourselves *in* the Lord. Remind yourself each day that strength doesn't come from your bank account, career, or any material thing. God is your source.

When you have some extra time, send an email to let me know how God is doing a work on your heart and in your life. I look forward to hearing some great man cave stories!

Endnotes

1   *Merriam-Webster,* "Second fiddle." Date of access: November 24, 2014 (http://www.merriam-webster.com/dictionary/secondfiddle).

2   Look up some other amazing second fiddle stories, such as Scotty Moore (guitarist for Elvis), Albert Einstein (second fiddle to William Hymanson), and Steve Ballmer (Bill Gates' first business manager).

3   *Merriam-Webster,* "Cowboy." Date of access: November 24, 2014 (http://www.merriam-webster.com/dictionary/cowboy).

4   *Goodreads,* "Corrie ten Boom Quotes." Date of access: November 24, 2014 (http://www.goodreads.com/author/quotes/102203.Corrie_ten_Boom).

5   *Naomi's Village,* "Our Name." Date of access: November 26, 2014 (http://naomisvillage.org/the-name/).

6   *What Does My Name Mean?* "Mara." Date accessed: November 17, 2014 (http://what-does-my-name-mean.org/name/mara/).

7   *Wikipedia,* "Boll Weevil Monument." Date of access: November 18, 2014 (http://en.wikipedia.org/wiki/Boll_Weevil_Monument).

8   *Wikipedia,* "Ted Williams." Date of access: November 24, 2014 (http://en.wikiquote.org/wiki/Ted_Williams).

9   Jeremy Camp, *I Still Believe* (Carol Stream, IL: Tyndale House Publishers, 2013).

10   Bob and Debby Gass, *The Word for Today,* "Come to God's City of Refuge." March 4, 2014 (http://www.thewordfortoday.com.au/index.php?option=com_blog_calendar&&year=2014&month=03&day=04&modid=89). Quoting Max Lucado.

11   *BrainyQuote,* "The time to relax..." Date of access: November 24, 2014 (http://www.brainyquote.com/quotes/quotes/s/sydneyjha152325.html).

12   *Goodreads,* "Quotable Quote." Date of access: November 25, 2014 (http://www.goodreads.com/quotes/230266-sometimes-i-sits-and-thinks-and-sometimes-i-just-sits).

13   *Goodreads,* "Quotable Quote." Date accessed: November 19, 2014 (http://www.goodreads.com/quotes/609132-you-know-the-smallest-thing-can-change-a-life-in).

About the Author

40 Days in the Man Cave has been a dream in the works for a number of years and is Todd's first published book. Todd has written published devotions for *Stand Firm* magazine of Nashville, Tenessee. Todd is an extremely gifted artist who recently illustrated a children's book, *The ABC's of God's Character*. In 2013, he collaborated with his wife Sherry, providing the illustrations for her devotional with study guide, *Water in the Desert* (second edition available through Word Alive Press). Todd and Sherry are stepping out as they pursue their God given dreams encouraging men and women to 'Take the 40 Day Challenge' through their devotionals. Todd has a raw, unique way of writing and within the book has included some powerful art he created that is both personal and significant leaving an imprint on your heart and mind.

Todd loves the adrenaline rush and camaraderie of his career as a North American certified First Class Firefighter. He has proudly served his community since 2004. Todd is happily married to Sherry, Christian author, speaker, and blogger who has a love for fast cars and grew up working at her family-operated drag strip!

HEART SURGERY AT LONDON UNIVERSITY HOSPITAL,
LONDON, ONTARIO, CANADA, SEPTEMBER 22, 2014

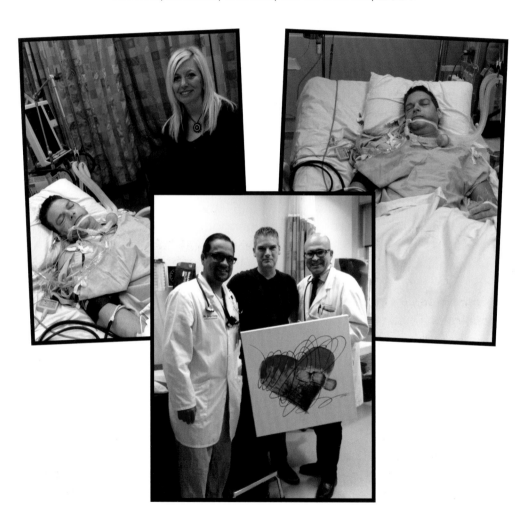

CURIOUS? TO READ ABOUT THE AMAZING STORY AND THE SIGNIFICANCE OF THE ART,
PLEASE GO TO MY WEBSITE AT WWW.TODDSTAHL.COM